Photography

Selected from the
Graphis Annuals

PAGE ONE PUBLISHING

Cover: Miko Lajczyk

Works selected from original titles »Graphis Photo«
© 1989, 1990, 1991, 1992, 1993 by
Graphis Press Corp., Dufourstr. 107, CH - 8008 Zürich

© 1994 for this edition: Page One Publishing Pte Ltd, Singapore
Distributed worldwide by
Könemann Verlagsgesellschaft mbH
Bonner Str. 126, D - 50968 Köln

Designed by Peter Feierabend, Berlin
Foreword by Carola Stoiber, Berlin
English translation by Karen Williams, Wall
French translation by Sylvie Adam-Kuenen, Cologne
Typesetting by Zentralsatz Dieter Noe, Cologne
Printed and bound by Toppan Printing

Printed in Singapore
ISBN 981-00-5719-9

Foreword

This book guides the viewer through the various genres of photographic art. Each genre has a different appeal, and where we choose to linger will depend on our personal taste and current mood. Today, perhaps, we may simply wish to bask in the beauty and expanse of the landscapes of Newfoundland and Australia (pp. 102/104); tomorrow, on the other hand, we may be ready to confront the misery of the world's crisis flashpoints.

The chapter devoted to »Journalism« presents a selection of photographs which bring us face to face with aggression, hunger, fear and power. The moment at which a masked South Korean student draws back his arm to hurl a home-made Molotov cocktail at an invisible opponent is captured by press photographer Heeson Yim (p. 92). His colleague Jim Sims focusses on victims of politics: on p. 94 he takes us to El Salvador, where he portrays a young woman fighting for the rebels. Her machine gun is leaning against the bench on which she is sitting, a young village boy beside her.

Alongside the sometimes shocking, often suppressed reality encountered in these photographs, however, there is also comedy and black humour. Who could help smiling at the sight of a goose perched on top of a motor cyclist's helmet (p. 133)? Or two penguins waddling past in the distance – across an expanse of ice as flat as the horizon (Bruno J. Zehnder, p. 128).

There can be a comic element to fashion photography, too, which presents its more eccentric side on p. 14. Here, H. Ross Feltus invites children to play at being grown-ups, clothing them in the dresses and suits designed for their mothers and fathers. He places a rolling-pin and a bottle of champagne in the hands of his little big models in order to reinforce the image. For another shot – children advertising children's clothes – he gives them carrots and dolls (p. 15). Even in his commissioned works, Feltus transmits his own independent, personal message: »Feed them a healthy diet and give them freedom – not just to play.«

In the photographs by Gottfried Helnwein, on the other hand, it is the setting which speaks loudest. Beneath a hammer and sickle, he stands a Russian woman in a heavy uniform next to a blonde in a figure-hugging one-piece dress (p. 31). Hard lines on the left and soft contours on the right. With this photograph, Helnwein – one of the most important and most controversial artists of the present day – not only shows the contrast between Socialist and Western ideals (of beauty), but offers us a portrait of the age. However great the differences between them though, these women are holding hands.

The scenery changes again with the transition to still life. The focus suddenly shifts to objects, and a photographic fascination with the interplay of the colours of a flower, the shape of a fruit, or the overall composition: sugared almonds in a chequered mug and on the scalepan (Antal Farkas, p. 51). Why was the glass of wine simply left standing, its last mouthful undrained? And who was the last person to wear the coat whose worn leather and gaping holes speak of rain, snow, hectic days and long nights? There is so much life behind these objects by Stefano Bianchi and Jonathan Lovekin (pp. 38/39) that the viewer is moved to formulate his own possible answers in his mind. And thus he suddenly quits the usual consumer passivity – imagination begins to take over.

Vorwort

Dieser Band führt durch die verschiedenen Genres fotografischer Kunst. Mit welchen sich der einzelne Betrachter länger beschäftigt, hängt ganz von persönlichen Vorlieben und Launen ab. Heute will er vielleicht einfach nur die Weite und Schönheit der Landschaften Neufundlands oder Australiens (S.102/104) genießen; morgen ist er bereit, sich mit dem Elend in Krisengebieten auseinanderzusetzen.

Das Kapitel Journalismus zeigt eine Auswahl an Fotografien, die unmittelbar mit Aggression, Hunger, Angst oder Macht konfrontieren. Die Sekunde, in der ein vermummter, südkoreanischer Student ausholt, um eine zu einem Molotow-Cocktail umfunktionierte Flasche auf seine unsichtbaren Gegner zu werfen, hielt der Presse-Fotograf Heeson Yim fest (S. 92). Sein Kollege Jim Sims porträtierte »Opfer der Politik«. Mit ihm geht es auf S. 94 nach El Salvador, wo er ein junges für die Rebellen kämpfendes Mädchen traf. Ihr Maschinengewehr lehnt neben dem kleinen Dorfjungen, mit dem sie auf der Bank sitzt.

Aber nicht nur die manchmal schockierende und oftmals verdrängte Realität, auch Groteskes und Komisches wartet auf neugierige Augen. Wer möchte nicht einmal eine Gans auf dem behelmten Kopf eines Motorradfahrers bewundern (S. 133)? Oder zwei Pinguine in der Ferne vorbeiwatscheln sehen – auf einer Eisfläche, die so schnurgerade verläuft, wie der Horizont (Bruno J. Zehnder, S. 128).

Die Modefotografie präsentiert sich hier von ihrer ausgefallenen Seite. Kinder spielen das Erwachsensein, ziehen die Kleider und Anzüge an, die für ihre Mütter und Väter entworfen wurden (S. 14). Die Idee stammt von H. Ross Feltus, der seinen kleinen, großen Models Nudelholz und Sektflasche in die Hände legte, um den Ausdruck noch zu verstärken. Für eine andere Aufnahme – Kinder werben für Kinderkleidung – gab er ihnen Karotten und Puppen (S. 15). So übermittelt Feltus auch bei Auftragsarbeiten seine eigenen unabhängigen, persönlichen Botschaften: »Ernährt sie gesund und gebt ihnen Freiraum – nicht nur zum Spielen.«

Gottfried Helnwein läßt dagegen vor allem die Inszenierung sprechen. Unter Hammer und Sichel stellt er eine Russin in klobiger Uniform neben ein blondes Mädchen im figurbetonten, einteiligen Kleid. Strenge Linien links und weiche Konturen rechts. Mit diesem Foto auf S. 31 zeigt einer der bedeutendsten und umstrittensten Künstler der Gegenwart nicht nur den Kontrast zwischen realsozialistischen und westlichen (Schönheits-)Idealen, er liefert auch ein Porträt der Zeit. Und erinnert auf seine Weise an die Aufgaben jener, die sie miterleben. Mag der Gegensatz auch groß sein, diese Mädchen halten sich an den Händen.

Eine andere Grenze wird mit dem Übergang zum Thema Stilleben überschritten. Plötzlich stehen Gegenstände im Mittelpunkt der Aufmerksamkeit, fasziniert das Zusammenspiel der Farben einer Blüte, die Form einer Frucht, die Komposition: Dragees im karierten Becher und auf der Waagschale (Antal Farkas, S. 51). Warum wurde das Glas mit dem kleinen Rest Wein einfach stehen gelassen? Und wer könnte den Mantel zuletzt getragen haben, dessen abgewetztes Leder und klaffende Löcher Geschichten von Regen, Schnee, hektischen Tagen und langen Nächten erzählen? Hinter den von Stefano Bianchi und Jonathan Lovekin auf der Doppelseite 38/39 dargestellten Objekten steckt soviel Leben, daß der Beobachter im Geiste mögliche Antworten in Form von ganz eigenen Bildern entwickelt. Und so verläßt er plötzlich seine passive Position als Konsument – die Phantasie beginnt zu spielen.

Préface

Cet album passe en revue les différents genres de l'art photographique. Chacun s'arrêtera plus longtemps sur l'un ou sur l'autre en fonction de ses préférences et de ses dispositions personnelles. Aujourd'hui, un tel voudra peut-être simplement se laisser charmer par l'étendue et la beauté des paysages de Terre-Neuve ou d'Australie (pages 102 et 104); demain, il sera prêt à regarder le malheur qui règne dans les points chauds du globe.

Dans le chapitre consacré au journalisme, une sélection de photographies décrit carrément l'agression, la faim, la peur et le pouvoir. La seconde, pendant laquelle un étudiant sud-coréen masqué s'apprête à lancer sur un adversaire invisible une bouteille transformée en cocktail molotov, a été fixée par le photographe de presse Heeson Yim (page 92). Son collègue, Jim Sims, a fait les portraits des «victimes de la politique». Page 94, il nous entraîne au Salvador où il a rencontré une jeune rebelle. La mitrailleuse de celle-ci repose en appui près d'un petit villageois qui est assis à côté d'elle sur le banc.

Mais ce n'est pas seulement la réalité ici et là choquante et souvent refoulée qui attend l'œil du curieux, c'est aussi le grotesque et le comique. Qui ne souhaiterait pas au moins une fois admirer une oie sur la tête casquée d'un motocycliste (page 133)? Ou bien voir dans le lointain deux pingouins se croiser en se dandinant sur une banquise aussi rectiligne que l'horizon (Bruno J. Zehnder, page 128).

La photographie de mode se montre ici sous un aspect inédit. Les enfants jouent aux adultes, portent les vêtements et les ensembles conçus pour leurs pères et mères (page 14). On doit cette idée à H. Ross Feltus, qui a mis dans les mains de ses modèles, petits et grands, un rouleau à pâtisserie et une bouteille de mousseux pour faire encore plus d'effet. Sur une autre photographie – où des enfants posent pour des vêtements d'enfants – il leur a donné des carottes et des poupées (page 15). Ainsi, même lorsqu'il s'agit de travaux exécutés sur commande, Feltus transmet tout de même son message personnel: «Nourris-les bien et laisse-leur les coudées franches – pas seulement pour jouer.»

Gottfried Helnwein, par contre, laisse avant tout parler sa mise en scène. Il fait poser sous le marteau et la faucille une Russe en uniforme grossier près d'une jeune fille blonde revêtue d'une robe moulante. Sévérité des lignes à gauche et douceur des contours à droite. Avec cette photo, à la page 31, l'un des artistes les plus importants et les plus controversés d'aujourd'hui ne se contente pas seulement de montrer le contraste entre les idéaux (de beauté) du socialisme réel et ceux de l'Occident. Il délivre en même temps le portrait d'une époque. Tout en rappelant, à sa façon, les devoirs de ceux qui la vivent. Aussi différentes qu'elles soient, les deux jeunes filles se tiennent les mains.

Une autre frontière est franchie lorsqu'on arrive à la nature morte. Soudain les objets deviennent le centre d'intérêt; l'accord parfait des couleurs d'une fleur, la forme d'un fruit, la composition fascinent: des dragées dans un gobelet à carreaux posé sur le plateau d'une balance (Antal Farkas, page 51). Que fait ici ce verre au fond duquel il reste un peu de vin? Et qui a bien pu porter en dernier ce manteau dont le cuir fatigué et les trous béants racontent la pluie, la neige, les journées fébriles et les longues nuits? Les objets que présentent en double page (38 et 39) Stefano Bianchi et Jonathan Lovekin recèlent une telle vitalité, que l'observateur donne comme réponses possibles des tableaux entièrement concus dans sa tête. Du coup, il abandonne sa passivité de consommateur. Son imagination se met en branle.

Javier Vallhonrat

Javier Vallhonrat

Hans Hansen

Rick Rusing

Steven Meisel

Steven Klein

H. Ross Feltus

H. Ross Feltus

Martin Riedl

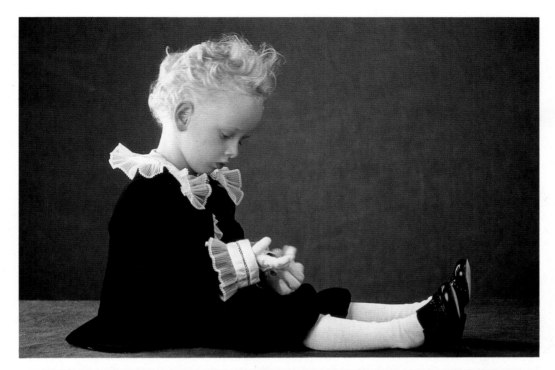

Frank Horvat

Yann Arthus

Aldo Fallai

William Hawkes

Sheila Metzner

Daniel Wreszin

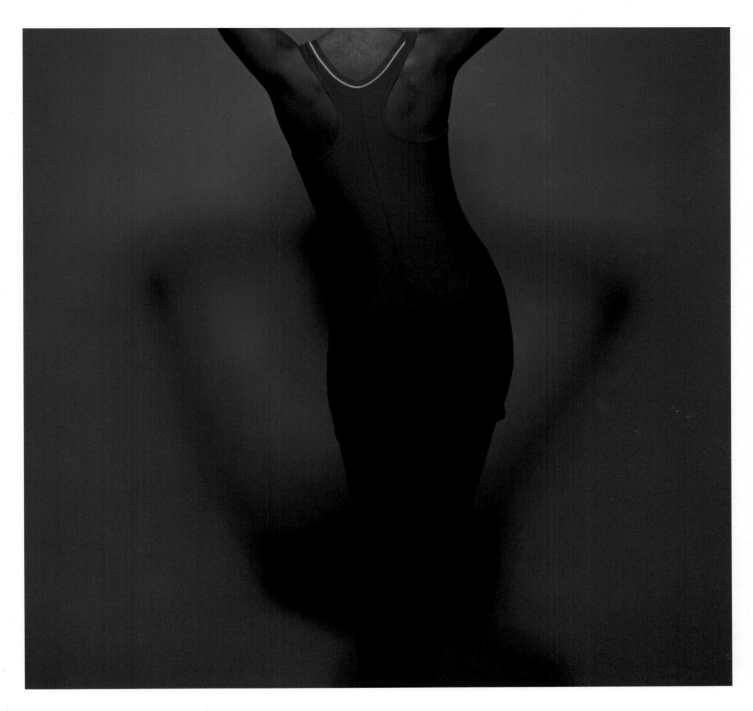

Robert Quick

Rodney Smith

Joyce Tenneson

Alan David-Tu

Jean-Baptiste Mondino

Miko Lajczyk

Minsei Tominaga

Fabrizio Gianni

Albert Watson

Monika Robl

Hornick/Rivlin Studio

Darrell Peterson

Stefano Bianchi

Jonathan Lovekin

André Baranowski

Terry Heffernan

Kathryn Kleinman

Douglas Benezra

Patience Arakawa

Parish Kohanim

Jan Oswald

Eugenia De Olazabal

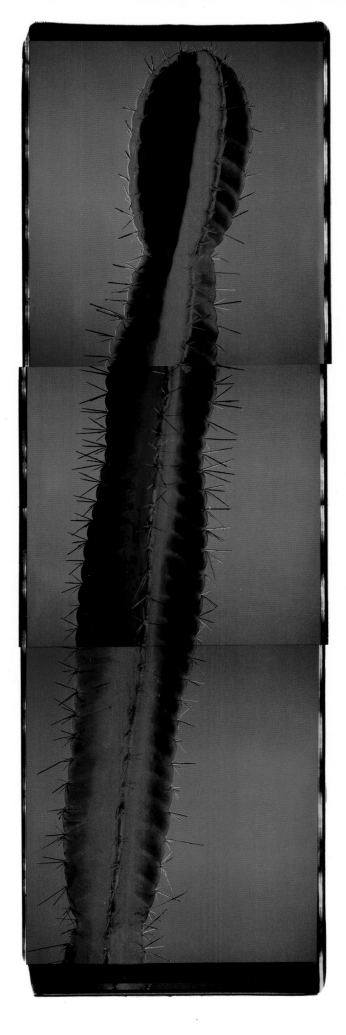

Thomas Hollar

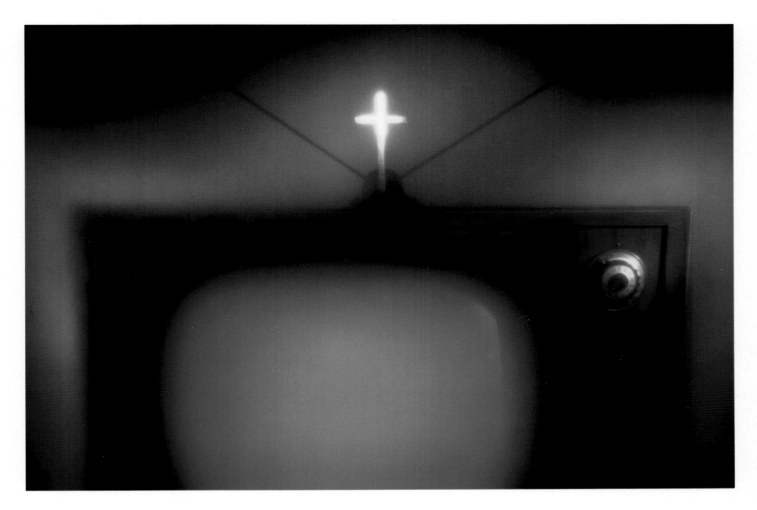

Mark Wiens

Luca Perazzoli

Antal Farkas

Paul Franz-Moore

Fernando Luiz

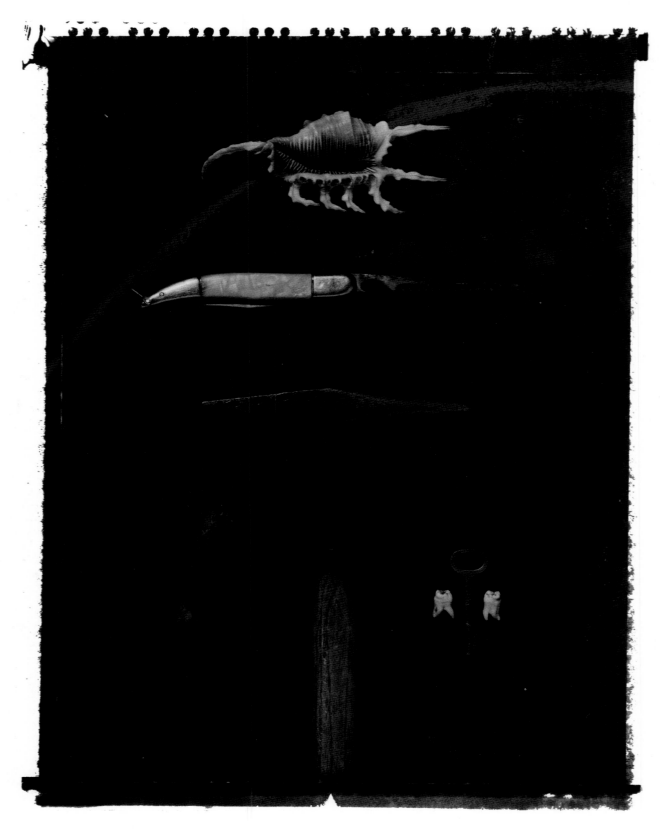

Ron Baxter Smith

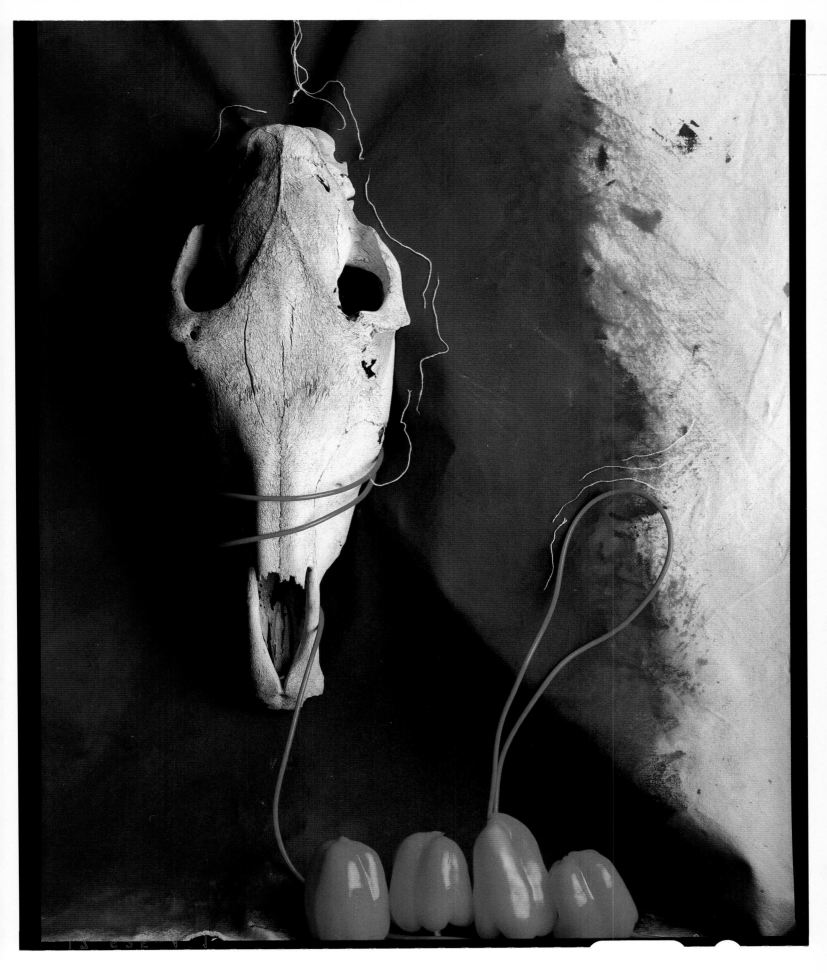

Philip Bekker

John Payne

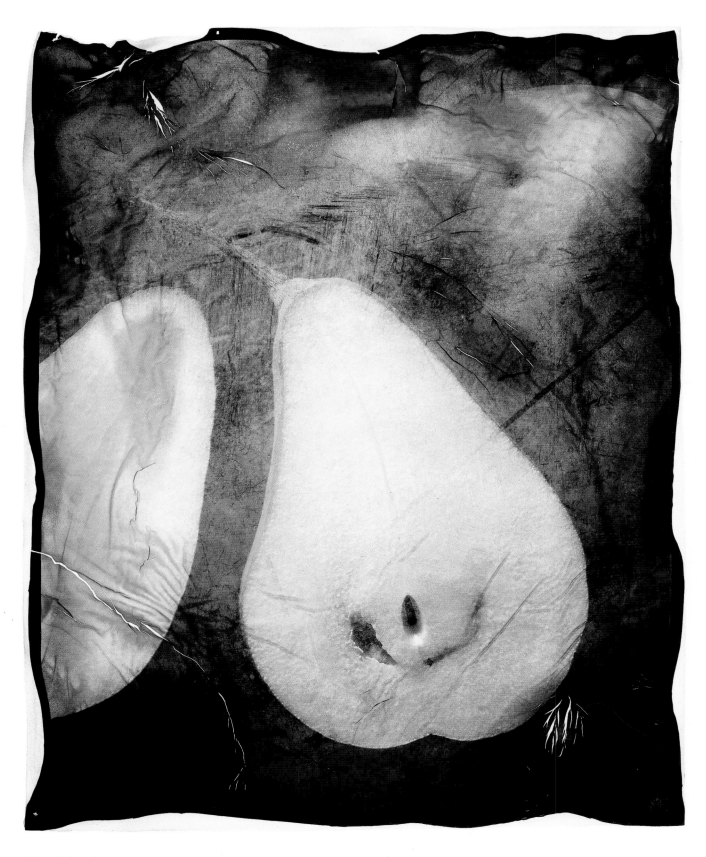

Rahmesh Amruth

Ken Matsubara

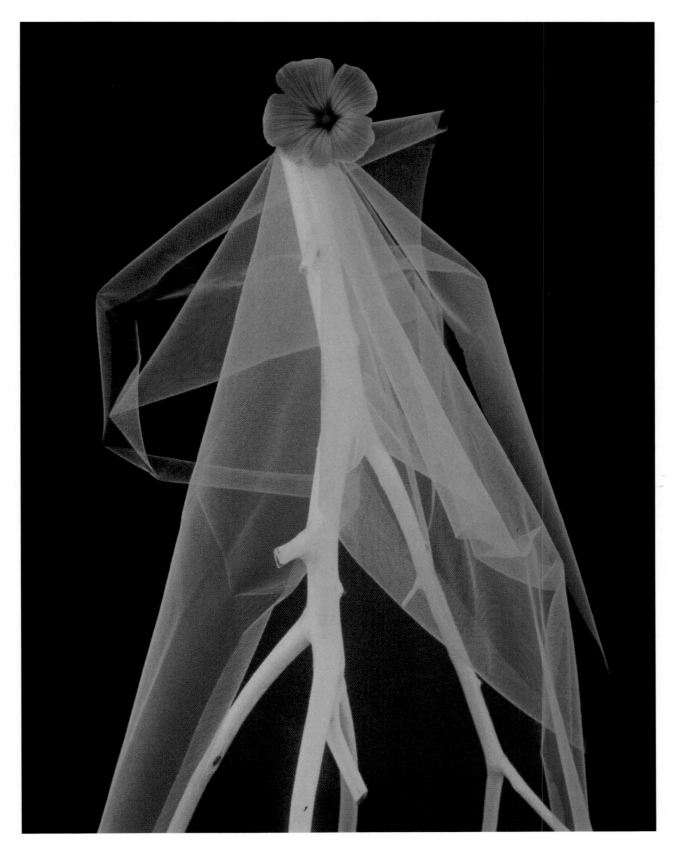

Alfons Iseli

Terry Heffernan

Conny J. Winter

Tom Vack/Corinne Pfister

◁◁ Steve Sharp

◁ Nadav Kander

Michael Furman

William Wegman

Dennis Manarchy

George Kamper

Rodney Rascona

Rick Rusing

Andreas Marx

Hans Hansen

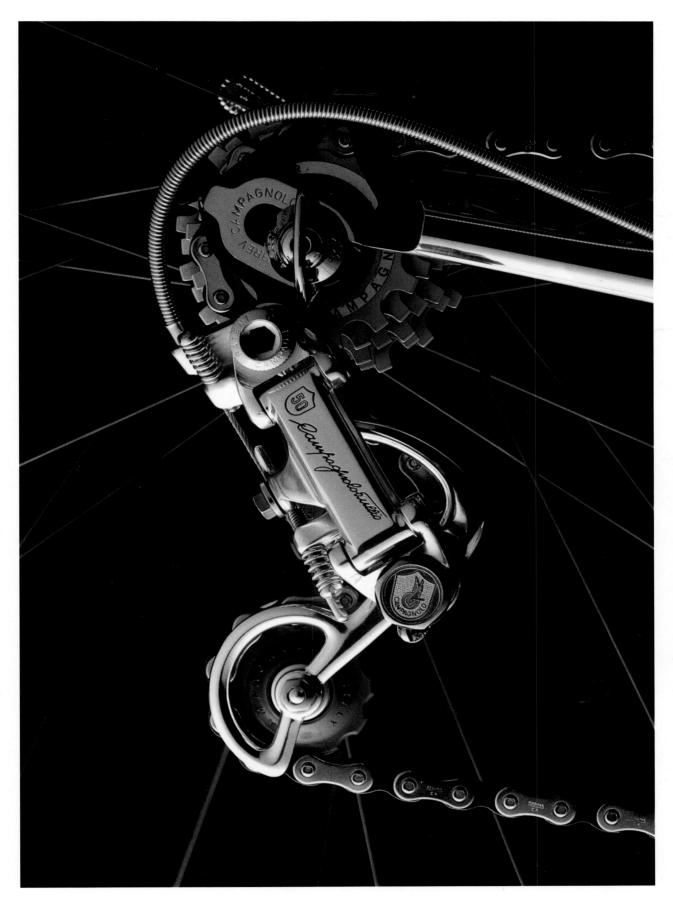

Michael Furman

Rick Rusing

Nikolay Zurek

Stefan Kirchner

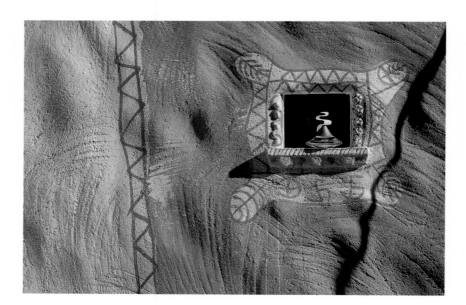

Stefan Kirchner

Stefan Kirchner

John Payne

John Payne

Michael Northrup

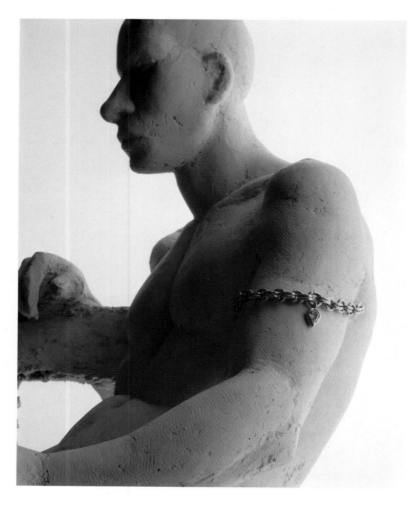

Dietmar Henneka

Harry Wade

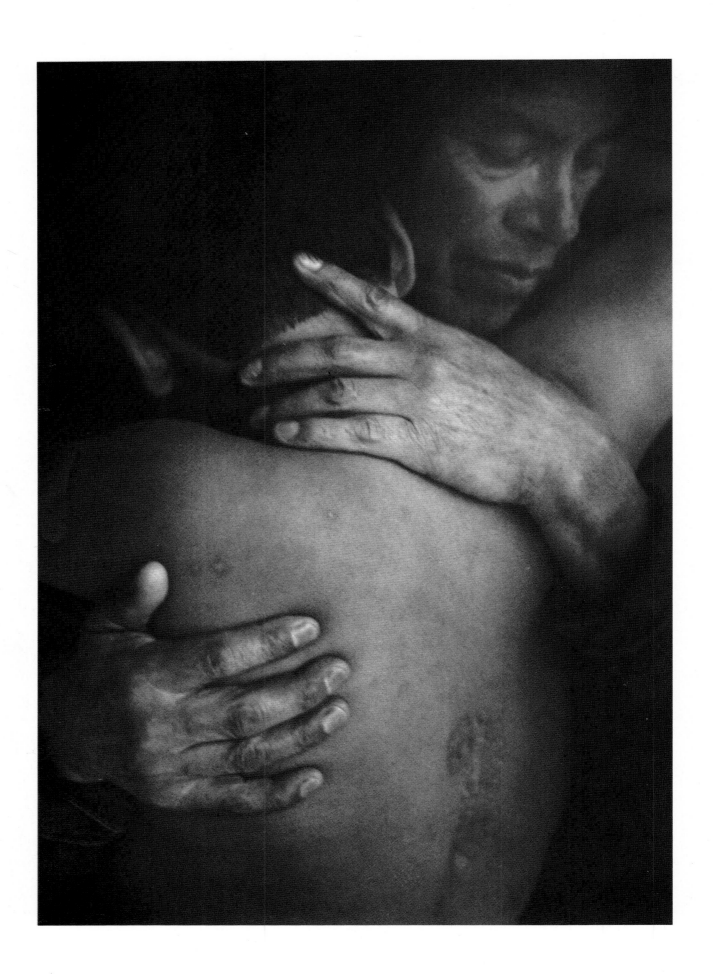

Boris Yurchenko

Soviet army tanks line up near the Russian Parliament in a brief show of force, ending in a peaceful and rapid retreat.

Aufnahme aus *Newsweek*: Eine kurze Machtdemonstration sowjetischer Panzer vor dem russischen Parlament im Jahre 1991 endete mit einem schnellen friedlichen Rückzug.

Les chars soviétiques, qui avaient pris place devant le Parlement russe en 1991 après la tentative de putsch, se retirent rapidement et dans le calme.

Charlie Cole/Picture Group

South-Korean police with riot shields during a demonstration in Masan in 1987.

Südkoreanische Polizei mit Schutzschildern bei einer Demonstration in Masan, 1987.

Police sud-coréenne armée de boucliers pendant une manifestation à Masan en 1987.

◁◁◁ Raymond Meeks

Hands that tell of suffering. This image, from a series of victims helped by Amnesty International was taken in Guatemala. Here, a father gently embraces his son who was paralysed from the waist down by a sniper's stray bullet, which had been intended for the father.

Raymond Meeks fotografierte für Amnesty International Hände von Opfern, denen von AI geholfen wird. Hier die Hände eines Vaters, der seinen querschnittgelähmten Sohn umarmt. Er wurde von einer Kugel getroffen, die wahrscheinlich seinem Vater gegolten hatte.

Raymond Meeks a photographié pour Amnesty International des mains de victimes, auxquelles AI vient en aide. Ici, ces mains sont celles d'un père qui étreint son fils. Ce dernier a été atteint d'une balle qui était probablement destinée à son père et il est devenu paraplégique.

◁◁ Ronald Olshwanger

Ronald Olshwanger is an amateur photographer who has been following fire trucks with a camera for 30 years. His picture of firefighter Adam Long rescuing an unconscious two-year-old girl has won him the Pulitzer Prize for spot-news photography.

Ronald Olshwanger, ein Amateur-Fotograf, folgt seit 30 Jahren mit seiner Kamera der Feuerwehr. Seine Aufnahme dieses Feuerwehrmanns, der ein bewußtloses zweijähriges Mädchen aus den Flammen rettete, wurde mit dem Pulitzer Preis ausgezeichnet.

Ronald Olshwanger est un photographe amateur qui, depuis 30 ans, photographie des interventions de sapeurs-pompiers. Cette photo d'un pompier sauvant des flammes une fillette de deux ans évanouie a été récompensée par le prix Pulitzer.

2

James Nachtwey/MAGNUM

»Point Blank«, photograph taken by a photojournalist for use by Kodak in an advertising campaign for *Kodak Professional Film*.

»Point Blank«, Aufnahme eines Fotojournalisten, die von Kodak für eine Werbekampagne für *Kodak Professional Film* verwendet wurde.

«Point Blank», par un reporter photo – cliché utilisé par Kodak pour une campagne de publicité en faveur du *Kodak Professional Film*.

Joel C. Freid

Pictures of a journey through Eastern Europe. »Baggage Woman«, »Radiator Boy«, and »Suceava North« were taken in Suceava, Romania. »Early Morning« (below right) was taken in Cracow, Poland.

Bilder einer Reise durch Osteuropa: »Gepäckfrau«, »Heizungsjunge«, »Suceava Nord«, alle in Suceava, Rumänien, aufgenommen. »Früher Morgen« (unten rechts), Krakau, Polen.

Images d'un voyage en Europe de l'Est: «bagagiste», «préposé au chauffage», «Suceava Nord» – 3 photos de Suceava, Roumanie. «Tôt le matin» (en bas à droite), Cracovie, Pologne.

Emmanuel Angelicas

The nightlife of Bangkok, taken by Australian photographer
Emmanuel Angelicas: the girl Chiab and her 45; Fis from
the Crush Velvet Lounge; girls from the Fire-House Bar,
and a self-portrait with an M.16.

Das Nachtleben von Bangkok, gesehen von dem Fotografen Emmanuel Angelicas: Chiab und ihre 45er, Fis von
der Crush Velvet Lounge, Mädchen der Fire-House Bar
und ein Selbstporträt mit einer M.16.

La vie nocturne à Bangkok vue par le photographe australien Emmanuel Angelicas: la fille Chiab et son calibre
45, la jeune Fis du Crush Velvet Lounge, les filles du
Fire-House Bar et un autoportrait avec un M.16.

Christiane Marek/Christoph Seeberger

Beer tent at the Munich October Festival – photograph
from the book »Munich – City in Light«.

Bierzelt am Oktoberfest – Aufnahme aus dem Bildband
»München – Stadt im Licht«.

Pavillon de la bière au Festival d'octobre de la bière. Photo
figurant dans l'album «Pleins feux sur Munich».

Heesoon Yim/Agence France Presse

Photograph of a South Korean student armed with a bottle
to be used as a Molotov cocktail. The jacket and scarf is
the typical uniform of radical students.

Ein südkoreanischer Student, bewaffnet mit einer zu einem
Molotow-Cocktail umfunktionierten Flasche. Die Jacke und
das Tuch sind die typische Uniform der radikalen Studen-
ten.

Etudiant sud-coréen brandissant une bouteille agencée en
cocktail Molotov. La veste et le foulard caractérisent l'uniforme des étudiants radicaux.

Marcel Crozet/Diffusion Editing

Leap from the window. Photograph taken by an amateur photographer.

Sprung aus dem Fenster – Aufnahme eines Amateur-Fotografen.

Saut dans le vide – photo réalisée par un photographe amateur.

Jim Sims

An example of Jim Sims's documentary work in El Salvador: an adolescent girl who fights with the rebel forces photographed with a young child from an impoverished village.

Eine Aufnahme aus der Serie des Fotografen Jim Sims über die Opfer der Politik: ein halbwüchsiges Mädchen, das zu den Rebellen gehört, mit einem Kind aus einem Dorf in El Salvador.

Une photo du reportage sur les enfants du Salvador réalisée par Jim Sims: une adolescente, membre des commandos rebelles, photographiée avec un petit villageois.

John Vink

The circumstances surrounding this photograph are solemn, but not as tragic as the photo might suggest. The hanging feet belong to a child playfully hanging from a bar, while the girl makes rope for a hammock. The children are refugees political turmoil in El Salvador, living in the camp of Mesa Grande in San Marcos, Honduras.

Die Umstände dieser Aufnahme sind ernst, aber nicht so tragisch, wie man annehmen könnte. Die herabhängenden Füße gehören einem Kind, das sich von einer Stange hängen läßt, während das Mädchen ein Seil für eine Hängematte anfertigt. Die Kinder sind Flüchtlinge aus El Salvador, die im Lager Mesa Grande in San Marcos, Honduras, untergebracht sind.

Photo prise au camp des réfugiés Salvadoriens de Mesa Grande à San Marcos, au Honduras. Bien qu'assez dramatiques, les circonstances ne sont pas aussi tragiques que l'image le suggère: pendant que la jeune fille tord des fils pour confectionner les cordes du hamac, un enfant s'amuse à se suspendre par les bras dans le vide.

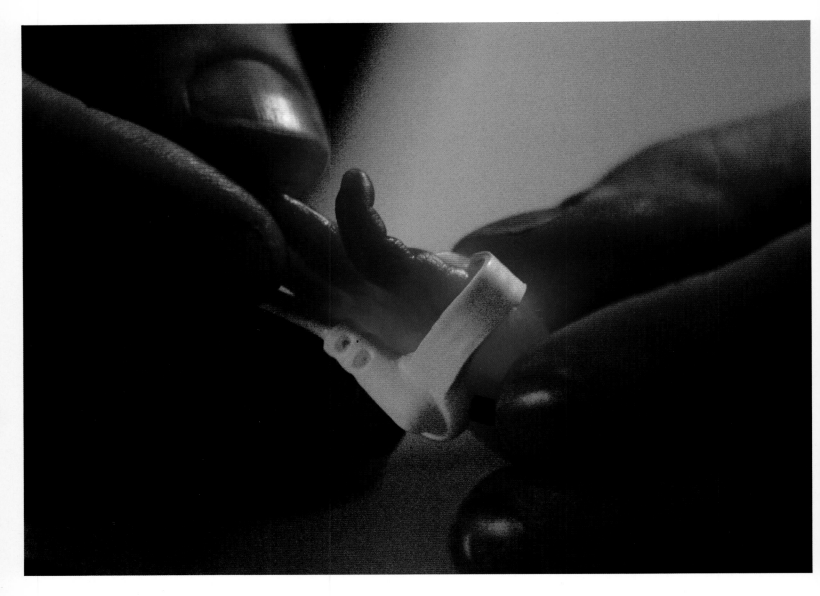

Thomas Stephan

Photograph of the tiny hand of a prematurely-born baby,
and the head of an instrument which continuously meas-
ures the current oxygen content of the blood by determin-
ing the absorption of red and infra-red wavelengths. From
a report in *Geo* about a doctor's struggle to save the lives
of quintuplets who were born three months prematurely.

Die winzige Hand eines extrem früh geborenen Kindes,
mit dem Meßkopf eines Instruments, das aus der Absorption von rotem und infrarotem Licht fortwährend den ak-
tuellen Sauerstoffgehalt des Blutes errechnet. Aufnahme
aus einem Artikel in *Geo*, in dem ein Arzt über den Kampf
um das Leben von Fünflingen berichtet, die drei Monate
zu früh zur Welt kamen

La main minuscle d'un prématuré, avec la tête de mesure
d'un instrument indiquant en continu la teneur du sang en
oxygène sur la base de l'absorption de lumière rouge et
infrarouge. Photo pour un article de *Geo* où un médecin
narre le combat mené pour maintenir en vie des quintuplés
venus au monde trois mois trop tôt, et la somme d'efforts
investie dans cette aventure.

Peter Turnley

A child from Eritrea, living in the Tug-Wajale refugee camp in Somalia, a country unable to provide substantial relief due to its own civil war. The girl is so weak from hunger that she has not the strength to brush away flies covering her body.

Ein Flüchtlingskind aus Eritrea im Tug-Wajale-Flüchtlings-lager in Somalia, wo wegen des dort herrschenden Bürger-kriegs ebenfalls Hunger herrscht, so daß man den Flücht-lingen kaum helfen kann. Das Mädchen ist zu schwach, um die Fliegen auf seinem Körper abzuschütteln.

Une fillette dans le camp de réfugiés érythréens de Tug-Wajale en Somalie où, à cause de la guerre civile, règne aussi la famine. La situation rend tout secours impossible. La fillette est trop faible pour chasser les mouches sur son corps.

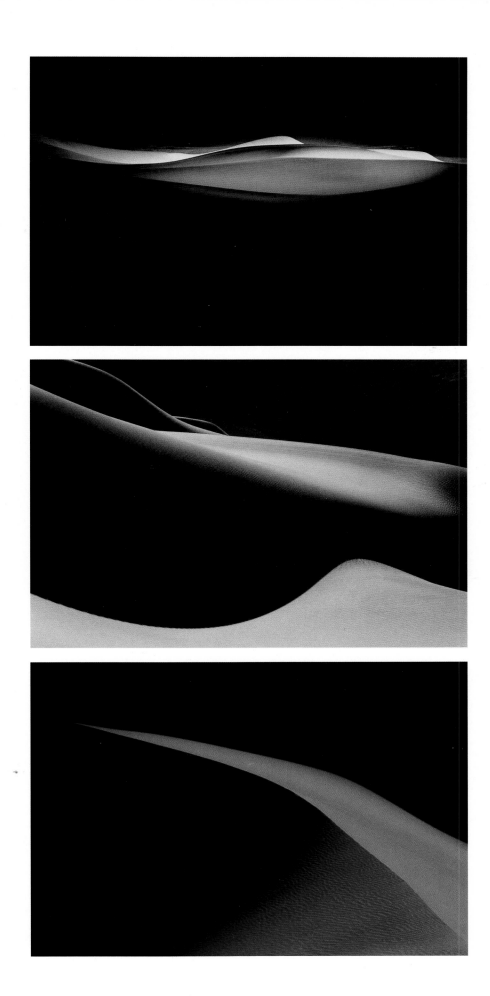

Arthur Meyerson

The destruction of the Amazon rain forest was the subject of an article in the client's company magazine. The project was supported by Wildlife Conservation International.

Die Zerstörung des tropischen Regenwaldes der Amazonasregion war das Thema eines Beitrags in der Firmenzeitschrift des Auftraggebers.

Réalisée pour une publication d'entreprise, cette photo, prise au Brésil, illustrait un article concernant la destruction de la forêt tropicale amazonienne.

◁ ◁ Nicolay Zurek

To contrast the old with the rebuilt portions of a steel mill in Ohio, black-and-white film was most suitable. The assignment was to generate art photographs of renovated plants, in colour, for office walls and the annual report of the client. This black-and-white image was taken »on the side«.

Der alte und der neue Teil einer Stahlfabrik in Ohio. Der Kontrast ließ sich am besten in Schwarzweiß herausarbeiten. Der Auftrag, bei dem es um die Modernisierung von Fabriken ging, verlangte Farbaufnahmen für die Büros und den Jahresbericht des Kunden. Dieses Schwarzweißbild entstand am Rande.

L'ancien et le nouveau bâtiment d'une aciérie dans l'Ohio. Le noir et blanc était particulièrement indiqué pour rendre le contraste. Le photographe devait faire des photos en couleurs de tous les sites rénovés de cette firme, afin de décorer ses bureaux ainsi que le rapport annuel. Cette photo a été prise en marge de cette commande.

◁ Intae Kim

Dunes at the Death Valley National Monument. The photographer waited patiently for the right light. The images are titled »Death Valley at Dawn« (top), »Dream in the Desert« (middle), and »Light of Symphony« (bottom).

Dünen im Death Valley National Monument. Der Fotograf wartete geduldig auf das richtige Licht. Er nannte seine Bilder »Das Tal des Todes im Morgengrauen« (oben), »Traum in der Wüste« (Mitte), »Das Licht der Symphonie« (unten).

Ces photos de dunes ont été prises sur le site du Death Valley National Monument. En haut: «La Vallée de la Mort à l'aube»; centre: «Le rêve dans le désert»; en bas: «La lumière de la symphonie». Pour chacun de ces clichés, le photographe dut attendre le moment où la lumière dessinait les formes les plus intéressantes.

Ron Bambridge

The photographer searched for an unusual landscape, which he found in Iceland with its black volcanic sand beaches, huge glaciers and icy peaks. This geothermal power station is set in a blue lagoon with hot springs where people swim.

Eine ungewöhnliche Landschaft hatte der Fotograf gesucht. Er fand sie in Island mit seinen schwarzen Lavastränden, riesigen Eiskappen und Bergkuppen. Dieses geothermische Kraftwerk befindet sich in einer Lagune mit heißen Quellen.

Le photographe désirait faire des vues de paysages hors du commun. C'est ainsi qu'il se retrouve en Islande, pays où l'on peut voir des plages de sable volcanique noir, des glaciers, des coulées de lave refroidies et des icebergs. Ici, les habitants se baignent dans les eaux réchauffées par une centrale géothermique.

Christian Février

Eric Tabarly's Yacht »Côte d'Or« is shown close to an enorm-
ous iceberg not far from the coast of Newfoundland
during the transatlantic race Lorient/St. Pierre-et-
Miquelon/Lorient. Photographer Christian Février captured
this image while sitting in a small fishing boat that was
leaking very badly and came close to sinking on the way
back to shore. Luckily, Février is a sailor of thirty years'
experience.

Die Hochseejacht »Côte d'Or« von Eric Tabarly vor einem
riesigen Eisberg in der Nähe von Neufundland während
einer Transatlantik-Regatta von Lorient/St. Pierre-et-Mique-
lon/Lorient. Die Aufnahme wurde von einem kleinen
Fischerboot aus gemacht, das leck war und bei der Rück-
kehr beinahe sank. Der Fotograf Christian Février segelt
selbst seit 30 Jahren, und er schreibt für viele Jacht-
Magazine.

Le maxi-yacht d'Eric Tabarly, «Côte d'Or», près d'un énorme
iceberg non loin de Terre-neuve. Cette photo a été réalisée
pendant la course transatlantique Lorient/Saint-Pierre-et-
Miquelon/Lorient en 1987, à partir d'un petit bateau de
pêche qui prenait l'eau et qui faillit couler au retour. Le
photographe pratique la voile depuis 30 ans et collabore
à de nombreux magazines de yachting.

Bruno J. Zehnder

Iceberg and bird in the Antarctic. The sun was low. Photographer Bruno J. Zehnder waited in a small boat for the little bird to fly into the exact spot of light on the top of the iceberg. An unstable boat added adventurism to the enterprise.

Eisberg und Vogel in der Antarktis. Die Sonne stand niedrig am Horizont, und der Fotograf wartete in einem winzigen Boot, bis der kleine Vogel genau im Licht der Spitze des Eisbergs war. Bei der Aufnahme wäre das Boot fast gekentert.

Iceberg et oiseau dans l'antarctique. Le photographe, installé dans une petite barque, a dû attendre que l'oiseau soit juste dans la lumière. L'instabilité de l'embarcation rendit cette opération fort périlleuse.

Aernout Overbeeke

Photograph taken during a location hunt in Australia. The rocks pointing out of the water are called »The 12 apostles«.

Diese Aufnahme entstand während einer Location-Suche in Australien. Die aus dem Wasser ragenden Felsen werden »Die zwölf Apostel« genannt.

Photo réalisée en Australie, pendant la recherche d'un lieu pour faire des prises de vue. Les récifs sont appelés «Les 12 apôtres».

A portrait of a dog taken in the countryside near Stratford St. Mary, England.

Porträt eines Hundes, aufgenommen auf dem Lande in der Nähe von Stratford St. Mary, England.

Portrait d'un chien photographié dans la campagne de Stratford St. Mary, en Angleterre.

Stephen Wilkes

Photographs for a self-promotional piece for the photographer. The first was taken at Wellfleet, Massachusetts, the second at Glacier National Park, Montana.

Diese Aufnahmen entstanden in Wellfleet, im Staat Massachusetts, und im Glacier National Park, Montana, USA. Sie dienten als Eigenwerbung des Fotografen.

Photographies servant d'autopromotion au photographe. La première photo a été prise à Wellfleet, dans le Massachusetts, la seconde au Glacier National Park à Montana.

Art Kane

From an advertising campaign for the Sunday edition of
the English newspaper *Daily Mail*.

Aus einer Werbekampagne für die Sonntagsausgabe der
englischen Zeitung *Daily Mail*.

Campagne publicitaire pour l'édition dominicale du
quotidien anglais *Daily Mail*.

Nadav Kander

A cornfield after the harvest, photographed in the USA for
an ad campaign in which the durability of Dunham Boots
had to be communicated.

Ein abgeerntetes Maisfeld in den USA, fotografiert für eine
Werbekampagne für Dunham-Stiefel, deren Strapazier-
fähigkeit demonstriert werden sollte.

Un champ de maïs fraîchement moissonné aux Etats-Unis,
photographié pour une campagne de publicité pour les
bottes Dunham illustrant leur solidité.

Horst Munzig

The Blue Lagoon, Iceland's »biggest bath« is the catch basin of a power plant in the hot springs region of Grindavik.

Die Blaue Lagune, Islands »größte Badewanne«, ist das Auffangbecken eines Kraftwerks im Thermalgebiet bei Grindavik.

La Lagune bleue, «la plus grande baignoire» d'Islande, constitue le bassin de réception d'une centrale thermique près de Grindavik.

Peter Stone

This photograph was taken at Bondi Beach, Sydney, in a salt water swimming pool.

Diese Aufnahme entstand in einem Salzwasser-Swimmingpool an der Bondi Beach in Sydney.

Cette photo a été réalisée dans une piscine d'eau salée à Bondi Beach, Sidney.

Martin Kers

From an article about Brittany appearing in the Dutch magazine *Avenue*: a 19th century castle.

Aus einem Beitrag über die Bretagne in *Avenue*: ein Schloß aus dem 19. Jahrhundert.

Pour un article que le magazine hollandais *Avenue* a consacré à la Bretagne: château du XIXe siècle.

VISUM/Rolf Nobel

These days, a submarine in the Kiel Canal is a rare sight, although this canal was originally constructed for military purposes.

Ein U-Boot im Nord-Ostsee-Kanal, ein seltener Anblick, obgleich dieser Kanal ursprünglich für militärische Zwecke gebaut wurde.

Sous-marin dans le canal de Kiel qui relie la Baltique à la mer du Nord et qui fut creusé à l'origine pour des raisons militaires, alors qu'un sous-marin y est aujourd'hui des plus rares.

Yann Arthus-Bertrand

Photograph used as a double spread for an article in *Geo* about Venice. The Lido di Jesolo was once the epitomy of the stylish bathing life.

Als Doppelseite verwendete Aufnahme für einen Artikel über Venedig in *Geo*. Der Lido di Jesolo war einmal der Inbegriff des mondänen Badelebens.

Photo en double page illustrant un article que *Geo* a consacré à Venise. Le Lido di Jesolo fut jadis le symbole de la vie balnéaire de la société élégante.

Richard Misrach

Photograph from an article in the *Frankfurter Allgemeine Zeitung* entitled »Myths of Sand and Stone: The Desert«. Richard Misrach took the shots in Southern California. He shows a desert whose temporary inhabitants have left their traces.

Aufnahme aus einem Artikel im *Frankfurter Allgemeine Magazin* mit dem Titel »Mythos aus Sand und Stein: Die Wüste«. Richard Misrach fotografierte im südlichen Kalifornien; er zeigt eine Wüste, die vom Menschen gezeichnet ist.

Photo tirée d'un article du *Frankfurter Allgemeine Magazin* intitulé «Mythes de sable et de pierres: le désert». Richard Misrach les a réalisées dans le sud de la Californie. Il montre un désert que l'homme a marqué de sa griffe.

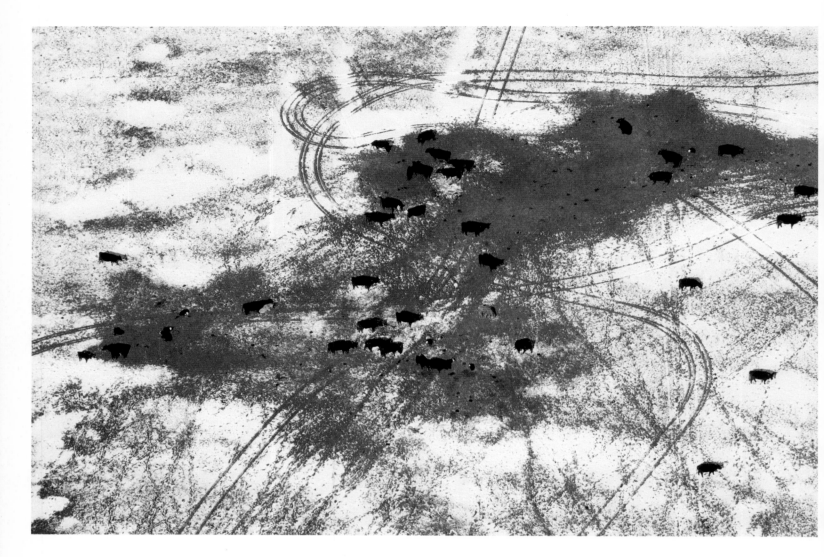

Robert Llewellyn

Snow-sugared prairie like a vast gingerbread, raisined with feeding cattle.

Wie Puderzucker liegt der Schnee auf der Prärie; die weidenden Rinder wirken wie Rosinen.

La neige saupoudrant la prairie évoque un pain d'épice où le bétail représenterait les raisins secs.

John Isaac

This dramatic scene, which has the look and feel of a painting was photographed during the traditional »Fantasia« fete of Morocco. John Isaac, who calls this his favourite photograph, waited for the right moment and angle as the sun was setting.

Diese dramatische Szene, die wie ein Gemälde wirkt, wurde beim traditionellen marokkanischen »Fantasia«-Fest von John Isaac festgehalten. John Isaac machte die Aufnahme bei Sonnenuntergang, im richtigen Moment, im richtigen Winkel.

La charge des cavaliers lors d'une «Fantasia», fête marocaine traditionnelle, évoque certaines peintures de batailles. Le photographe, John Isaac considère cette photo comme l'une de ses préférées. Il l'a réalisée pendant le coucher du soleil.

Gerrit Buntrock

Les Szurkowski

Reinhart Wolf

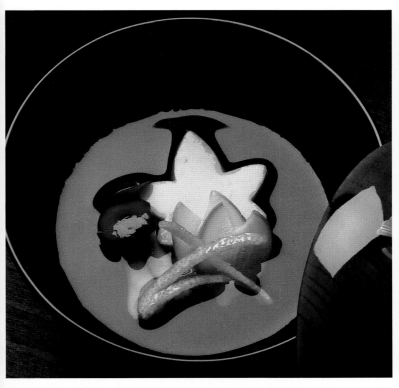

Francois Gillet

Paul Franz-Moore

Michael Wissing

Rosanne Olson

Michael Wissing

Philip Bekker

Achim Schroten/Georg Schreiber

John Parker

Bruno J. Zehnder

Hugo A

Britta Jaschinski

Friedrich K. Rumpf

Adrian Burke

◁◁ Curt Fischer

◁ Bill White

Teiji Saga

Jim Brandenburg / National Geographic Society

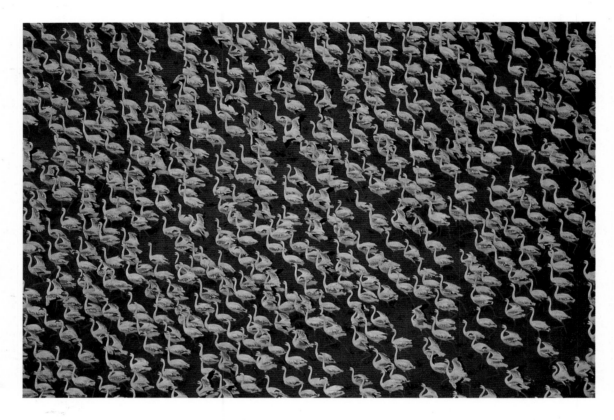

Frans Lanting

John Claridge

Tim Griffith

Wayne Cable

Miquel Gonzales

Greg Pease

Christoph Seeberger

Doug Keats

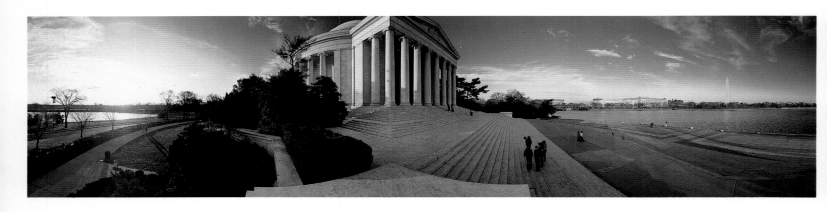

Marc Segal

Alain Janssens

Jay Maisel

Richard Hamilton

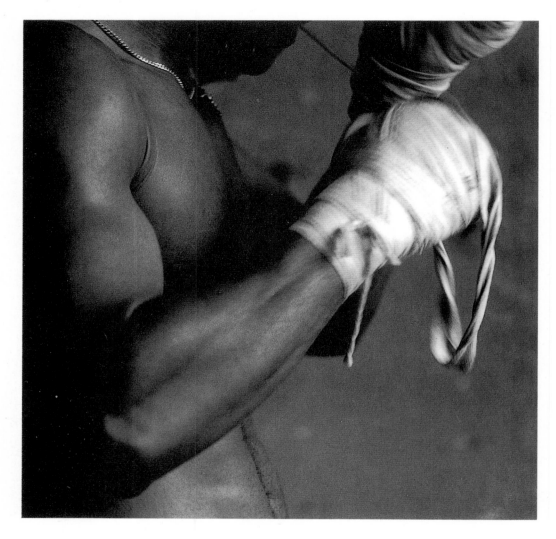

Mark Ferri

Robert Mizono

Laci Perény

Tim Bieber

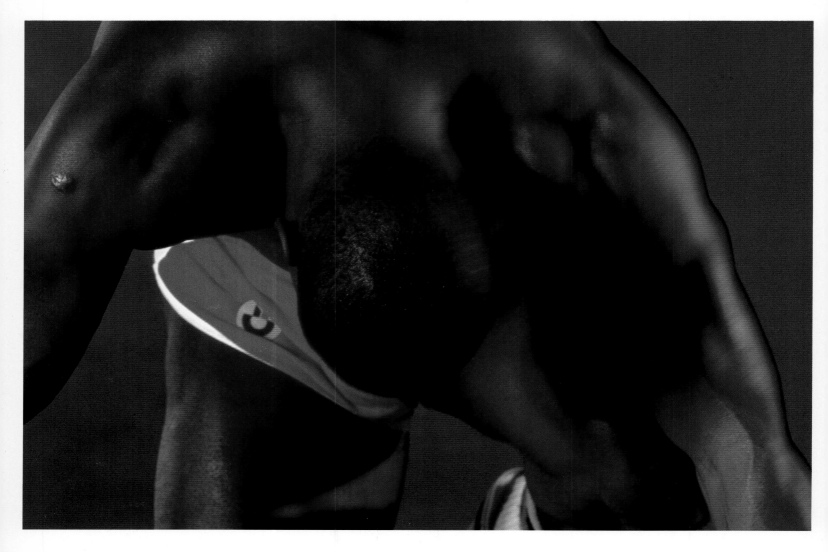

Peter Ginter

Gregory Heisler

Oliver Strewe/Wildlight

Reinhard Klein/SIPA